IMAGE
of Amer

LOCKHEED

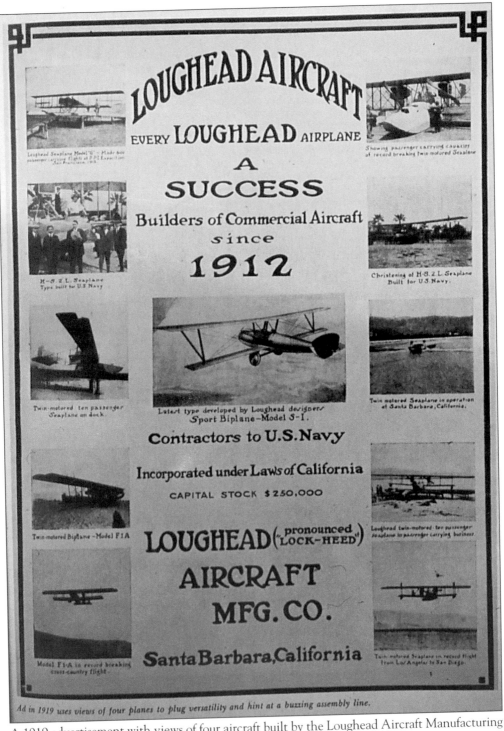

Ad in 1919 uses views of four planes to plug versatility and hint at a buzzing assembly line.

A 1919 advertisement with views of four aircraft built by the Loughead Aircraft Manufacturing Co.

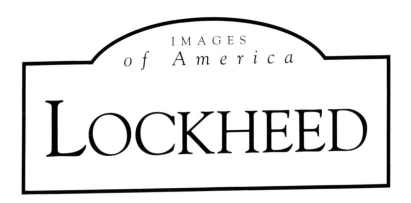

IMAGES
of America

LOCKHEED

Compiled by
Martin W. Bowman

TEMPUS

First published 1998
Copyright © Martin W. Bowman, 1998

Tempus Publishing Limited
The Mill, Brimscombe Port,
Stroud, Gloucestershire, GL5 2QG

ISBN 0 7524 1536 0

Typesetting and origination by
Tempus Publishing Limited
Printed in Great Britain by
Midway Clark Printing, Wiltshire

Malcolm (left) and Allan Haines Loughead at the controls of their 1916 F-1 flying boat, which they reconverted into a land plane (F-1A) in 1918.

Contents

Acknowledgements

The author would like to thank: Alan Brothers; Mike Bailey; Ray A. Crockett; Brian Foskett; David Grimer; Terry Holloway; Stephen Jefferson; Mick Jennings; Lockheed-Martin Corp.; Peter Mallinson; Marshall Aerospace; Brian McGuire; Jerry C. Scutts; Graham M. Simons; Hans Heri Stapfer; the dedicated staff of the US 2nd Air Division Memorial Library in Norwich; Derek S. Hills, Trust Librarian; Linda J. Berube, American Fulbright Librarian; Lesley Fleetwood; Christine Snowden. All were most helpful and provided much willing assistance with research.

In 1916 the Loughead Aircraft Manufacturing Company produced two Curtiss HS-2L single-engined flying boats. Pictured with one of them are: Malcolm Loughead in the gun turret with, in front, Norman S. Hall, Anthony Stadlman, Burton R. Rodman, Allan Loughead and John K. 'Jack' Northrop. Unfortunately, both the Curtiss boats were built at a loss.

Introduction

In the early 1900s, Malcolm and Allan Haines Loughead, two young aviation-minded brothers in San Francisco, California, started out with the help of their half brother, Victor, on the road that was to lead two of them to form one of the biggest aviation corporations in the world. Allan Loughead, a fine engineer, aircraft designer and pilot, and newly married, returned to San Francisco early in 1912 where he resumed work as a mechanic. He managed to convince Malcolm, who for the past eight years had worked as an automobile mechanic (designing the famous hydraulic brake in the process), that they should build their own aircraft, the Model G. In 1912 they set up the Alco Hydro-Aeroplane Company from a garage at Pacific and Polk Streets in San Francisco. At the same time they continued to work as automobile mechanics to help finance the construction of the Model G.

During the summer of 1913 the Model G made four flights before it was damaged in an accident at San Mateo. Allan and Malcolm bought out the interests of their fellow investors and acquired the Model G outright. In 1913 they were forced to seek their fortune by prospecting in the California gold country. After a year of prospecting, followed by several exciting adventures at home and abroad, Malcolm and Allan moved to Santa Barbara in 1916, and together with other investors, they created the Loughead Aircraft Manufacturing Company. With the help of an architectural draughtsman by the name of John K. 'Jack' Northrop, the Lougheads built an F.1 flying boat and produced two Curtiss HS-2L single-engined flying boats. Unfortunately, both the Curtiss boats were built at a loss, a small S-1 sport biplane failed to penetrate a market dominated by war-surplus Jennies and a Navy contract for fifty scouts was cancelled before the first aircraft was completed. In 1921, the company went into liquidation and Jack Northrop went to work for Douglas.

On 13 December 1926 the Loughead brothers and other investors formed the Lockheed Aircraft Company. Fred E. Keeler, a wealthy brick manufacturer, acquired fifty-one per cent of the common stock and took the title of president. Allan Loughead was vice-president. With the help of Jack Northrop, now Chief Engineer, Lockheed designed and built the trend-setting Vega cantilever monoplane, which was sold (at a loss) to George Hearst Jnr, the wealthy San Francisco newspaper magnate. The company is, however, best remembered for building what were arguably the fastest, finest and most sought after

Between the wars a total of 128 Vega 1s, 2s and 5s were built, including 115 by Lockheed, and nine by Detroit, while 149 Model 10 Electras were built. Pictured is Amelia Earhart's 10-E Electra NR16020, in which she disappeared in July 1937, with grey-blue Vega 1 NC199E *Elizabeth Lind*, manufactured on 20 January 1929.

monoplanes of the period 1927-34. Their unique single-shell wooden monocoque construction put their Vega and Orion cabin planes well ahead of their competitors' fabric-covered biplane designs. The speedy, high-winged Vegas in the hands of accomplished trail-blazers like Amelia Earhart, Ruth Nichols and Wiley Post completed many long-distance flights and set new speed records, while the most famous owner of a Lockheed 8 Sirius was Charles Lindbergh, who completed a number of survey flights around the world for Pan American Airways in 1930 and 1933. A Lockheed 3 Air Express won the 1929 National Air Race and a year later the same aircraft, in the hands of Roscoe Turner, set a number of new speed records.

In March 1928, meanwhile, the Lockheed company had moved its offices to the Mission Glass Works in Burbank, where four Vegas, an Air Express and an Explorer were built. (The Explorer, which was designed for long-distance record attempts, was the least successful of the early Lockheed aeroplanes. Just four were built, of which three crashed. The fourth was damaged and parts from this aircraft were mated to an Orion fuselage to produce the Orion-Explorer in which Wiley Post and Will Rogers were killed in Alaska on 15 August 1935.) Jack Northrop left the company three months later. He was replaced by Gerald F. 'Jerry' Vultee as chief engineer. By mid 1929, well over seventy Vegas, seven Air Expresses and the Explorer had either been built or were under construction. Keeler saw that this was the time to realize a large profit and against Allan Loughead's wishes, in July 1929 a deal was made with the Detroit

One of Lockheed's greatest contributions to the Second World War was the manufacture of 2,941 Hudson bombers, military versions of the Model 14 Super Electra airliner. Over 1180 Hudsons were delivered to the RAF under pre-war British contracts and Lend-Lease agreements.

Aircraft Corporation who snapped up eighty-seven per cent of Lockheed's assets. Just three months later the Wall Street crash plunged the US into the Great Depression and many companies went into liquidation.

The Lockheed Aircraft Company was a division of the Detroit Aircraft Corporation for two years until it too went into receivership. During this sojourn, Lockheed carried on producing Vegas, Air Expresses and Explorers as well as building new designs, the most famous of which was the Sirius, the first being completed for Charles Lindbergh in 1929. In addition, a number of Altair and Orion aircraft were built. On 21 June 1932 at a bankruptcy court a group of investors led by Robert E. Gross, a San Francisco investment broker, bid $40,000 for the assets of the defunct company. There being no other bids, Judge Harry Holzer accepted their offer, adding, 'I sure hope you fellows know what you're doing.' Gross became chairman and treasurer of the new Lockheed Aircraft Corporation, while Lloyd C. Stearman was elected president and general manager.

The new regime saw Lockheed move away from single-engined to twin-engined designs, the first of which was the successful Model 10 Electra transport, followed in due course by the Model 12 Electra Junior fast executive transport. In 1936, Lockheed delivered its first military aircraft to the US Navy, Coast Guard and AAC, and plant facilities were increased to build the Model

Burbank turned out 9,924 P-38 (Model 22) Lightnings (P-38J-10-LO 42-68008, pictured). The L was the final production version and 2,520 copies were built.

14 Super Electra, which would fly on 24 July 1937. Also conceived at about this time was the XP-38 (Model 22) twin-engined interceptor, which was submitted to meet AAC requirement X-608 in February 1937. Destined to become famous as the Lightning, its designers were Hall Hibbard, and twenty-seven-year-old Clarence L. 'Kelly' Johnson. Johnson had advised the company about potential instability and control problems on the Model 10 and had joined the company as a tool designer in 1933. Model 22 development was protracted, with the revolutionary turbo-superchargers causing the most delays, and the XP-38 did not fly until 27 January 1939. In the meantime, Lockheed tried hard to carve a niche in the highly competitive transport market with the Models 10, 12, 14 and later 18 transports. There then came a breakthrough on 23 June 1938, when Britain placed an order for 200 to 250 Hudson aircraft.

The Second World War saw Lockheed grow enormously. On 31 March 1940, the workforce stood at 7,000 employees, and in 1941 it had risen to 16,898 personnel. Between 1 July 1940 and 31 August 1945 Lockheed turned out 19,077 aircraft to become the fifth largest US aircraft producer. By far the largest proportion of Lockheed-built aircraft were Lightnings, Hudsons, and Lodestars, although 500 B-17F and 2,250 G Fortresses as well as B-34/37 and PV-1/-2s were produced at Burbank by the Vega Corporation (formerly

During the Second World War Lockheed-Vega turned out 3,028 Ventura and Harpoon bomber versions of the pre-war Lodestar 18. The biggest user of the Ventura was the RAF, which received 675 Mk I and Mk II versions, while the US Navy operated the bulk of PV-1 and PV-2 Harpoons.

AiRover Company), which was absorbed on 30 November 1943. Just over 94,300 personnel, thousands of them women engaged in building aircraft on the production lines, were working at Lockheed at this time.

After the war, Lockheed sought other markets, notably in the field of civil and military propeller-turbine and jet transports. In 1955 the Model 188 Electra turbine-powered airliner entered the design stage after American Airlines had showed their dissatisfaction with Douglas and the pricing of their DC-7 airliner by announcing that it was ready to receive bids for alternative aircraft for its hitherto Douglas-equipped fleet. On 8 June 1955 American Airlines ordered thirty-five Electras and on 27 September Eastern Airlines ordered forty. By the end of 1955 Lockheed had received orders for another sixty-one Electras. The Model 188 was completed in twenty-six months and flew, eight weeks ahead of schedule, on 6 December 1957. Airline deliveries began in 1958 but three Electras were lost in fatal accidents in fourteen months in 1959-60, and the company was forced into an expensive modification programme. Weakness of the engine mountings, which in turn caused nacelle vibration and then wing flexing and final failure at the root, was deemed to be the cause of at least two of the accidents, and although the problem was finally overcome, a loss of public confidence in the Electra signalled its demise. A military development, the P-3 (P3V) Orion long range patrol aircraft, however, went on to achieve great success.

Work on jet propulsion had started at the outbreak of war and the company's first jet fighter, the XP-80, was contracted by the USAF in June 1943. At the beginning of the programme, Kelly Johnson organized his famous Advanced Development Projects Section, which was housed in temporary

The XF-104 first flew on 4 March 1954 and proved so successful that ultimately 2,578 copies were built by Lockheed and under licence in Europe, Canada and Japan. No fewer than 1,127 were F-104Gs, 915 of which (including thirty F-104Fs) resulted from a decision by West Germany, in 1958, to re-equip the Luftwaffe with Starfighters.

accommodation next to a plastics factory. Its location earned the nickname 'Skunk Works', after the foul-smelling factory in Al Capp's *Lil Abner* comic strip. The name stuck. Completed in just 143 days, the XP-80 project exemplified Johnson's credo – be quick; be quiet; be on time. The P-80 became America's first production jet fighter, and by 1958 no less than 8,507 related models had been produced. Other successes included the Constellation family of turbo-prop transports, 856 of which were turned out, and a further 1,051 P2V Neptunes.

In January 1951 Lockheed re-opened a government-built plant at Marietta, Georgia, and the complex was used to build 394 Boeing B-47 Stratojets, C-130 Hercules and JetStar aircraft. The YC-130 prototype, which was to become famous as the Hercules, first flew on 23 August 1954. The type was to become hugely successful, while the Jetstar would continue in production until 1980. In 1961, the Lockheed-Georgia Division was reorganized as the Lockheed-Georgia Company.

Meanwhile, Kelly Johnson, named chief engineer at Burbank in 1952, and his design group at the famed 'Skunk Works', had turned their thoughts to other military jets. (The Advanced Development Projects Section later became the Lockheed Advanced Development Company, or LADC, and in the 1990s was responsible for building the F-117A Stealth fighter). Among the designs considered was the U-2 spy plane, and the Model 83, created in November 1952, which finally emerged as the F-104 Starfighter. It owed much to the

C-130E Hercules in Vietnam. The 'Herk' first flew in prototype form on 23 August 1954 and thirty-seven variants resulted. By 1994, 2,086 C-130 Hercules had either been built or were on order.

1940s design concept of the experimental Douglas X-3 Stiletto, which first flew on 20 October 1952, and which was built to investigate the design features of an aircraft suitable for sustained supersonic speeds.

In October 1958 the West German Government rejected a dozen other fighter designs in favour of the F-104G and placed an order for sixty-six F-104Gs on 6 February 1959. Some 915 Starfighters were eventually acquired for the Luftwaffe, 653 of them licence-built in Europe. World-wide Starfighter production eventually reached 2,583. Lockheed-California built 740 of these, the most widely used Mach 2 fighter aircraft ever built. All told, Starfighters were produced by manufacturers in seven countries and they equipped no less than fifteen air forces. The jet's career, though, was marred by a very high loss rate. Forty-nine out of 296 Starfighters operated by the USAF were lost and eighteen pilots were killed, and in 1960 the type was withdrawn from Air Defense Command. In south east Asia, eight F-104s were lost in action and another six were destroyed in operational accidents before the type was phased out of theatre. The F-104 suffered an even higher accident rate in NATO service. By 1967 the Luftwaffe had lost sixty-six F-104s and thirty-seven pilots killed. Altogether, the Belgian Air Force lost thirty-nine Starfighters, the Dutch Air Force forty-four and, by late 1982, the Luftwaffe had lost 252 F-104s.

In 1956 Lockheed offered to build two high-altitude aircraft fuelled by liquid hydrogen, and work began on two CL-400 aircraft. This project was cancelled,

Lockheed has always been at the forefront of aviation technology and the SR-71A, which resulted from the A-12 Mach 3-plus reconnaissance aircraft project, flew for the first time on 22 December 1964. Three Hudson Mk VI transports of No. 117 Squadron over the Western Desert.

Lockheed has an enviable reputation for producing a wide range of superlative civil and military aircraft types, including maritime aircraft such as the Neptune, Orion and S-3A Viking. The last named successfully met a US Navy requirement in August 1969 for an experimental carrier-based ASW aircraft and the first prototype flew on 21 January 1972. A total of 179 Viking production models followed.

however, in October 1957, but work progressed on a Mach 3-plus reconnaissance aircraft and twelve A-12 aircraft were built following a full design go-ahead in January 1960. The A-12 prototype flew on 24 April 1962 and the aircraft were used for operational CIA flights around the world, while thirty-eight GTD-21B reconnaissance drones were built. These were for launching from beneath the wing of specially-modified B-52Hs of the 4200th Test Wing, and some reports indicate that these drones were used over North Vietnam. For a time there was a strong possibility that the A-12 could be used to meet a requirement for a Mach 3-plus interceptor after the North American XF-108 Rapier was cancelled in September 1959. The A-12 was modified and renamed the YF-12A but the intended interceptor version never entered production. Meanwhile, in 1963 work had begun on a redesign of the A-12 for the strategic reconnaissance mission and the SR-71A was adopted. The SR-71 flew for the first time on 22 December 1964 and test pilot Robert J. Gilliland took the aircraft to Mach 1.5. Deliveries to Strategic Air Command started in January 1966, and thirty-two examples were built before production ceased in 1968.

In May 1962 Lockheed-Georgia received a definitive contract for 132 (later increased to 285) C-141 Starlifters, and in 1976-77 Lockheed were contracted to 'stretch' all existing Starlifters. In 1965, meanwhile, Lockheed-Georgia had also been awarded a contract to build 115 C-5 Galaxy jet transports, but in November 1969 this was reduced to eighty-one aircraft. Lockheed was already having to come to terms with problems with AH-56A Cheyenne helicopter production for the US Army, a project which was finally terminated in August 1972. It ultimately forced Lockheed out of the helicopter business forever.

Lockheed were more successful in 1969, winning the VSX competition with the resulting S-3A for the US Navy (the Viking would remain in production until 1978). The Lockheed Propulsion Company, meanwhile, encountered insurmountable problems with a solid-fuel engine for the Boeing Short Range Attack Missile, and the company was finally inactivated. Another highly expensive enterprise was the proposed L-2000 supersonic transport, which lost out to the Boeing 2707. At first there seemed no future for the three-engined (Rolls-Royce RB.211) L-1011 airliner, later named the TriStar, but Lockheed shrugged off the initial disappointment of losing out to the McDonnell Douglas DC-10, to land orders for 172 TriStars from four major US airlines. In 1971 Rolls-Royce Aero Engines were placed in the hands of the receivers and production of TriStars ceased immediately. Without Government help, the Lockheed Aircraft Corporation would have followed the British engine manufacturer into bankruptcy. Funds were forthcoming, but Lockheed faced many more financial and political setbacks until it entered profitability again in 1973.

Two years later, the 'Lockheed Bribes' scandal broke when the publication of a Lockheed company report revealed that $22 million in 'sales commissions' had been paid to foreign officials, including $1 million to Prince Bernhard of

After decades of producing transports and other types of aircraft, Lockheed returned to building fighter designs, and the F-117A became the first production combat type designed to exploit low-observable (LO) technology. During the Gulf War in 1991, more than forty F-117A Nighthawks, such as this one pictured through infra-red camera, flew over 1,200 missions, all without loss.

the Netherlands. The scandal rocked Lockheed Aircraft Corporation to its very foundations, and the chairman of the Board and the vice-chairman and president were forced to resign.

On 1 September 1977 the Lockheed Aircraft Corporation became simply the Lockheed Corporation but by the end of 1978 only four types of aircraft were still in production. At Burbank the plant was turning out P-3 Orion and L-1101 aircraft (in August 1983, Lockheed was forced to terminate TriStar production after 197 aircraft had been built), while at Marietta, the C-130 and JetStar II aircraft were still being produced. The 1,500th C-130 was produced in 1978 and in December 1979 the 500th P-3 came off the Burbank production lines. A new lease of life for the U-2 was found in 1980, when the production lines were reopened to build three new reconnaissance versions for the military and for NASA.

Stealth low-observable (LO) technology incorporating a radar-absorbent airframe gathered pace and would lead, ultimately, to the first flight of the F-19A Spectre early in 1982. Fifty-nine F-117A Stealth reconnaissance-attack aircraft, designed by Ben Rich and his team at the Lockheed Martin Skunk Works, were ordered and, by November 1988, fifty-two had been delivered to the USAF. F-117As were the first US Air Force combat planes to strike key targets in Iraq on 17 January 1991 at the start of the Gulf War. An estimated ninety-five per cent of primary 'Desert Storm' targets in Baghdad were destroyed by the Stealth fighters.

One
In the Ascendancy

Four Hudson Mk VI transports of No. 117 Squadron over the Western Desert.

Loughead Model G three-bay biplane, completed as a floatplane in 1913, and first flown by Allan Loughead on 15 June that year. Forced to place the aircraft in storage for two years, the Lougheads finally recouped much of their outlay on the aircraft by giving 600 passengers ten-minute joy rides for $10 a time during fifty days at the 1915 Panama-Pacific Exposition. In 1918 the framework was scrapped and the Kirkham six-cylinder engine was sold to Curtiss.

Preliminary design work on the F.1 (Flying Boat One) capable of lifting two pilots and eight passengers, was undertaken by Allan Loughead in 1916, with assistance from his brother Malcolm and Jack Northrop. Powered by two Hall-Scott liquid-cooled engines, the aircraft first flew on 28 March 1918. The US Navy cooled on its initial interest but, like the Model G, the F.1 earned revenue on $5 joy hops and it was later converted to an F.1A land plane. It was sold in 1920 to raise capital for the Lougheads' S-1 sports biplane.

Although the S-1 single-seat sports biplane was not a commercial success, because its purchase price was higher than brand new surplus Curtiss Jennies available in large numbers at knockdown prices, its wooden monocoque construction served the Lougheads well when they came to build their highly-successful Vegas.

The concrete monocoque mould in which Lockheed formed the two plywood half-shell fuselages of its early single-engined aircraft from the Vegas to the Orions.

Fuselage framework being readied for application of finished half-shells.

The first Vega high-speed cabin monoplane was built in Hollywood and was purchased by newspaper baron George Hearst Jnr who intended to enter it in the August 1927 Oakland to Hawaii air race. It first flew, from a nearby Inglewood hayfield, on Independence Day (4 July) 1927. Named *Golden Eagle* (NX913), it took part in the race six weeks later but disappeared without trace with pilots Jack Frost and Gordon Scott.

Despite the loss of the first Vega, the aircraft marked a turning point and 115 were built by Lockheed, with another thirteen being turned out by Detroit and others. X3903, the third Vega 1 built, was used by Captain Wilkins and Lt Carl Ben Eilson on the April 1928 Detroit News - Wilkins Arctic Expedition, the first trans-Arctic flight.

On 16 November 1928, in X3903, Captain Wilkins and Lt Carl Ben Eilson became the first to fly a plane over Antarctica.

Vega 5, X4769, was the first Wasp-powered Lockheed. Named *Yankee Doodle*, in August 1928 it became the first aircraft to be flown non-stop between Los Angeles and New York City in both directions.

Bright yellow Vega 5 NC7429 *The Tester*, built in 1928, the personal plane of Erle P. Halliburton (left). It was flown by Robert W. Cantwell (right) to win the Class C transcontinental air derby and Free-for-All in 1928. The aircraft was demolished in an accident, which killed the pilot and four passengers, on 18 April 1933.

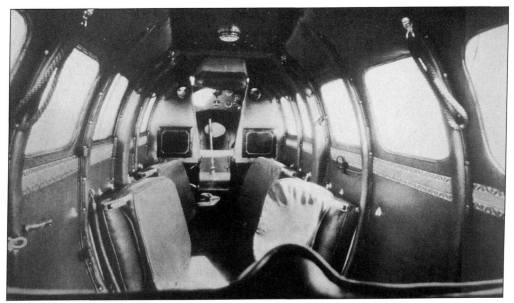

The cabin interior of a typical six-passenger Vega.

Vega 5 NR105W *Winnie Mae* (c/n 122), which was flown by owner F.C. Hall's personal pilot, Wiley Post. Post and Harold Gatty used it to make a record flight around the world in June-July 1931, while Post flew it solo around the world two years later. It was later modified for high-altitude experiments.

Vega 5 Special (c/n 619) NR496M with pilot Ruth Nichols, who established women's records in speed, altitude, and transcontinental flights in 1930-31.

Air Express 4897 (c/n 5) built for Western Air Express, Los Angeles, on show at a winter exhibition before going into airline service. The aircraft was badly damaged in a landing accident at Las Vegas during the second stage of its maiden flight to Salt Lake City on 6 June 1928, and was returned to Lockheed to be rebuilt.

4897 was retained by Lockheed (EX-2) and re-registered 7955. It was fitted with a new Wasp engine and became the first commercial aircraft built with a NACA cowling. On 4 February 1929 Frank Hawks and Oscar Grubb set a new coast-to-coast record in this aircraft. Altogether, seven Air Expresses were built.

Air Express 3 NR974Y (c/n 130) with Laura Ingalls, who made a solo circuit of South America in February-April 1934, for which she received the Harmon Trophy.

In 1929 Jerry Vultee adapted the Explorer design to create the high-performance Lockheed 8 Sirius (c/n 140/NR211) monoplane for Col. Charles A. Lindbergh. It was the company's first low-wing model, the first of fifteen Sirius built, and was initially powered by a 450hp Wasp engine. Lindbergh (seen here climbing into the cockpit) set a record west-to-east flight of 14hr 45min 32sec in 1930. Later fitted with a 575hp Wright Cyclone, and Edo floats, it was used on world survey flights in 1931 before it was damaged in China.

Charles A. Lindbergh pictured with Lloyd Stearman (standing) in 1933. A year earlier, Lockheed had rebuilt the Sirius as a land plane before re-installing the floats for the Lindberghs' 29,000-mile North and South Atlantic survey flights in late 1933. A 710hp Cyclone was fitted and the aircraft became the first Lockheed design to have sliding cockpit canopies. (Stearman had become president and general manager of Lockheed in June 1932 and he proceeded to design the Model 10.)

Five of the Sirius aircraft were converted to Lockheed 8 Altair Speedsters and these were followed by six more, one of which was assembled by the AiRover Company, and one built by Detroit. This sports-model design, the first Lockheed aircraft to be fitted with a retractable undercarriage, enabled Lockheed to meet the requirements of private fliers and commercial airline operators.

In 1932 Sirius c/n 152 was converted to Sirius 8 Special. In 1934 it was converted again, to an Altair 8D (VH-USB) with a new wing and a Wasp SE, to enable Sir Charles Kingsford-Smith to fly it in the MacRobertson Race between London and Melbourne. Originally named ANZAC, it had to be withdrawn, but between 21 October and 4 November 1934, Kingsford-Smith and his co-pilot, P.G. Taylor, flew the Altair 8D, now named *Lady Southern Cross*, on the first Australia-USA flight. They covered the 7,356 miles from Brisbane to Oakland, California, in less than 55 hours. Shipped to England in 1935 for a London-Melbourne flight attempt, *Lady Southern Cross* disappeared en route over the Bay of Bengal on 8 November with Kingsford-Smith and Tommy Pethybridge.

Varney Air Service Ltd (later Varney Speed Lanes Inc.) of Alameda, California, bought six Orion 9s (c/n 181/186, NC12223/12228). NC12225 *North Wind* carried passengers between San Francisco and Los Angeles between 1931 and 1934, on a schedule of 65 minutes, with an average speed of 254mph. This aircraft, and four of the others, later operated with Varney's Mexican airline. NC12225 and two of the other Varney Orions were among several used by the Republican Air Force in the Spanish Civil War in 1937.

Douglas Fairbanks, his wife Mary Pickford and the Maurice Chevaliers pose in front of Orion 9 (c/n 185), NC12227, *Winter Wind*, used by Varney from 1931 to 1934, before being transferred to Varney's Mexican airline, Lineas Aereas Occidentales SA. This Orion also ended up in Spain, being used by the Spanish Republican Air Force from 1937.

Orion 9D Special NR14222 (c/n 211) named *Auto-da-Fé*, in which Laura Ingalls set non-stop transcontinental records in November and December 1935 and came second in the 1936 Bendix race. The aircraft ended up in Spain in 1937 where it was used by the Republican Air Force.

Altair DL-2A (c/n 180) was converted to an Orion 9C Special (NR12222) in 1932 and sold to the Shell Aviation Corporation. It was piloted by Shell's Aviation manager, Jimmy H. Doolittle (pictured) on cross-country and exhibition flights.

The Detroit-Lockheed XP-900 (YP-24) of 1931 was Lockheed's first fighter, a joint effort between the erstwhile Detroit Aircraft Company and Lockheed. The two-seat aircraft became a casualty of the 1929 depression and a thirteen-plane contract was cancelled by the AAC in 1931. The XP-900 had a metal fuselage constructed in Detroit and was shipped to Burbank for final assembly with a California-made plywood wing.

The new regime saw Lockheed move away from single-engined designs to twin-engined machines, the first of which was the successful Model 10 Electra, of which 149 were built. One of the aircraft's most famous customers was Amelia Earhart, seen here posing on the nose of her 10-E Electra NR16020, in which she disappeared near Howland Island on 2 July 1937. Amelia had set several records in Lockheed Vegas in 1929-30 and 1932.

Following the success of its Electra, in 1936 Lockheed brought out a similar but smaller plane identified as the Model 12 (NC17374 of Superior Oil pictured). This was the fastest aeroplane of its size and type ever constructed in the US, and was intended for use by executives, corporations, feeder airlines, or sportsman pilots. The aircraft carried six passengers, pilot and co-pilot. The Model 12 found favour throughout the world because of its excellent flying characteristics, manoeuvrability, ease of handling, speed and low-cost maintenance. A total of 130 Model 12 Juniors was built.

Some 112 Model 14 Super Electra airliners were built by Lockheed (PJ-AIT, one of five Model 14-F62s for KLM, pictured) and another sixty-four by Tachikawa and fifty-five by Kawasaki in Japan. Several Lockheed innovations were introduced on the Model 14, which first flew on 29 July 1937, such as the single-spar, all-metal wing construction, the Lockheed-Fowler wing flap, and heavier wing loading. The result was an aircraft with higher speed and efficiency and increased safety. Howard Hughes circled the globe in a Model 14 in 1938, setting a record of 3 days, 19 hours and 14 minutes.

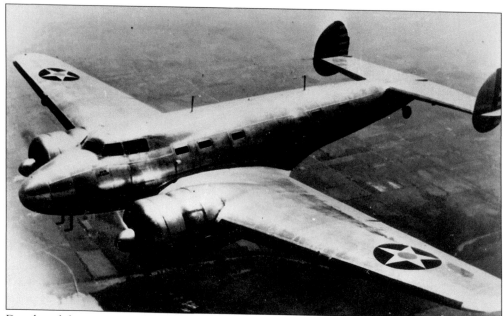

Developed for many months at Lockheed, the XC-35 (c/n3501) was the first aircraft with a pressurized cabin to fly in the sub-stratosphere, on 7 May 1937. A modified Electra, it had a nearly spherical fuselage reinforced internally. The AAC received the Collier Trophy in 1937 for its high-altitude flights in the XC-35, which pioneered later military and civil developments in pressurized flight.

On 22 April 1939 the six-place Vega Starliner (NX21725), designed to meet growing requirements of feeder airlines, flew for the first time, but the project was shelved when Vega turned to production of Venturas and B-17 bombers. Its 210mph speed was produced by a unique power plant arrangement of two in-line 260hp Menasco C6S-4 engines located side by side in the nose, geared to a single propeller.

A multi-purpose aircraft which entered service in 1940, the Model 18 Lodestar was used as an executive ship, airliner, cargo transport, flight research laboratory, and for many other commercial tasks. The normal passenger version carried fourteen people, plus a three-man crew, baggage and cargo. Some 625 Lodestars were built by Lockheed, plus a further 121 Ki-56 examples by Kawasaki in Japan. In the Second World War Lodestars were requisitioned as C-56 personnel, troop and freight transports.

BOAC operated thirty-eight Lodestars from 1941 to 1948, although only nine were ordered directly from Lockheed. The rest, including G-AGIL (pictured), were obtained from other airlines or from the RAF.

The Vega Model 35-70 version of the North American NA-35 primary trainer in flight in 1941. The aircraft was never destined to enter quantity production because first North American then Lockheed-Vega's production lines were taken up by other, more important, military designs, and only four were built.

The Model 14 Super Electra was converted to a military type to meet a British requirement in June 1938 for a coastal reconnaissance bomber and an order was placed for 200 Hudson Mk Is (N7280, from the first batch of 139, N7205/N7343, pictured) and as many more as could be delivered by December 1939, up to a maximum of 250. The Model B14L (Hudson Mk I/N7205) flew on 10 December 1938, at Burbank.

Eventually, 1,500 Hudsons were purchased for RAF Coastal Command and the RAAF before the bomber was included in Lend-Lease procurement programmes and became designated A-28. Some fifty-two A-28s and 450 A-28As were allocated to the RAF from AAC stocks. A Boulton Paul dorsal turret with two .303 machine guns (seen here atop T9303, a Hudson I of No. 206 Squadron) was installed after the aircraft arrived in Britain.

Hudsons first entered service with No. 224 Squadron at Gosport in the summer of 1939. When war broke out in Europe in September 1939 two squadrons, 224 at Leuchars, and 233 at Bircham Newton, were operational in Coastal Command. (A Hudson of No. 224 Squadron was the first RAF aircraft to destroy a German aircraft in the Second World War, on 8 October 1939). A third squadron, No. 220 (pictured), were in the throes of converting from the Anson to the Hudson at Thornaby.

A Hudson I of No. 206 Squadron taking off late in 1940.

A flak-damaged Hudson I of No. 220 Squadron back in England after an armed reconnaissance over Norway.

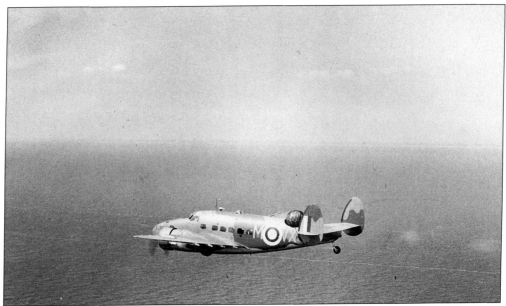

No. 206 Squadron Hudsons over Heligoland, 1940. 'M's top turret is firing at shipping (note the puffs), while taking return fire (there are two streaks of German tracer below).

A Hudson I of No. 206 Squadron being bombed up with 250-pounders (the Mk I could carry 750lb of bombs). Thirty-five Hudsons from Nos 59, 206 and 224 Squadrons took part in the second thousand-bomber raid on Bremen on 25/26 June 1942.

All told, 350 Hudson Is were built before production switched to the Hudson II (of which twenty were built), and these were followed by 414 Hudson IIIs. The first version supplied under Lend-Lease was the Hudson IIIA, 382 being delivered to the RAF (another 418 being diverted to the USAAC as the A-29). A total of 130 Mk IVs were built, mainly for the RAAF, followed by 309 Mk Vs for the RAF (Mk Vs of 48 Squadron are pictured). The last model for the RAF was the Mk VI transport with the turret removed. Production of the Hudson finished in May 1943 after 2,941 had been built.

In the summer of 1940 Britain placed an order for 188 Ventura Mk I bombers (plus a further 487 Mk IIs). The Ventura was a Vega military development of the Lodestar airliner. Two hundred Venturas, designated B-34, were serial numbered 41-38020/38219 for the USAAF but most of these were assigned to Britain under Lend-Lease in August 1941. The USAAF received twenty B-34-VEs upon the US entry into the war, and later ordered 550 B-37-LO versions, but only eighteen were ever built.

Lockheed Vega
advertisement for the
Ventura bomber.

AE658 was the first production Ventura, and flew on 31 July 1941. It differed from the Hudson in having Double Wasp engines, a dorsal turret positioned further forward to give a better field of fire, and a ventral gun position under the fuselage.

Ventura Mk I AE661 prior to delivery to No. 487 Squadron RNZAF. RAF crews dubbed the new bomber the 'Flying Pig' because of its porcine fuselage and said that the only thing it could do that the Hudson could not was consume more petrol!

Venturas equipped Nos. 21 and 464 RAAF and 487 RNZAF Squadrons in 2 Group, Bomber Command, and were used on suicidal daylight operations. Losses were high. This 21 Squadron Ventura (AE784), which crashed in the Waddensee on 6 November 1942, was one of three lost this day.

On 6 December 1942 2 Group mounted its biggest operation of the war when ninety-three light bombers, including forty-seven Venturas, attacked the Philips radio and valve works at Eindhoven from low level. Fourteen aircraft – nine of them Venturas – failed to return.

King George VI and Queen Elizabeth visiting No. 487 Squadron RNZAF at Methwold on 26 May 1943.

On 3 May 1943 'Ramrod 16' was mounted to encourage Dutch workmen to resist German pressure in Holland. Six Bostons of 107 Squadron bombed the Royal Dutch Steelworks at Ijmuiden, while twelve Venturas of 487 Squadron RNZAF (pictured at Methwold), led by twenty-eight-year-old Squadron Leader Leonard Trent DFC, RNZAF 'B' Flt Cdr (front row, centre, with hands crossed without gloves), were sent on a diversion to bomb the Amsterdam power station, escorted by three Spitfire squadrons. One Ventura aborted *en route* after losing the escape hatch. The other eleven, including Trent's, ran into a Schwarm of 2./JG27 and twenty-eight Fw 109A-4s of II./JG1 from Woensdrecht, led by Gruppenkommandeur Hptm Dietrich Wickop, who picked off ten of the Venturas in just a matter of minutes. Trent saw his bombs overshoot the power station before he too was hit. Trent's Ventura went into a spin and broke up. Two crew died trapped inside but Trent and one other crewman were hurled out of the aircraft. They survived and were taken prisoner. It was only after they were repatriated that the full story became known and on 1 March 1946, Trent was awarded the Victoria Cross for his leadership and gallantry.

On 22 June 1943 Ventura AE910 of No. 21 Squadron flown by W/Cdr H.S. King, the CO, was shot down by flak north-east of Abbeville Drucat. All five airmen on board were killed.

Ventura I AE660 of No. 21 Squadron.

Ventura I *Go To Return* of No. 487 Squadron RNZAF. Some forty-eight Venturas were lost and the type was finally retired from Bomber Command after July 1943, when it was relegated to Coastal Command duties.

'Look to Lockheed for Leadership' advertisement.

The rest of the Ventura production run (1,935 aircraft) was allocated to the US Navy as PV-1 (pictured) and PV-2 Harpoon aircraft, seeing widespread service, mainly in the Pacific, on over-water patrol operations. The Ventura was allocated to the US Navy on 24 July 1942 and some 1,600 PV-1s were delivered from December 1942 to May 1944. Included in this figure are 380 models sent under Lend-Lease to Britain as Ventura GR5s. Fourteen PV-1s were delivered to Australia, and New Zealand received 116 PV-1s and four PV-2s.

On 30 June 1943 Lockheed received an order for 500 PV-2s and service deliveries began in March 1944. The PV-2 had a greater wing area, longer range, seven machine guns (including five in the nose), a new tail and was able to carry up to ten .5 inch rockets and 4,000lb of bombs or torpedoes. PV-2s equipped fourteen US Navy squadrons and was first used in April 1944 from Attu in bombing and rocket strikes on Japanese positions in the Kuriles. The final variant was the PV-2D, of which 414 were ordered, though only thirty-five were constructed before the contract was cancelled.

Burbank turned out 9,924 P-38 (Model 22) Lightnings. This is the first, the XP-38-LO 37-457, pictured at March Field, California, which won Design Competition X-608 in February 1937. The XP-38 flew for the first time on 27 January 1939 at March Field, and was written off in a crash on 11 February 1939.

On 27 April 1939 a contract for thirteen YP-38s was placed and a year later the Anglo-French Purchasing Committee ordered 667 aircraft (Model 322), specifying that they were to have unsupercharged Allison V-1710 engines, so as to conform to the same power plant used on the Curtiss H-81A (P-40).

After the fall of France in June 1940, Britain took over the entire contract, now made up of 143 Lightning Is (AE979, the second Lightning I, pictured), and 524 Lightning IIs. However, testing in the UK proved unsatisfactory and a contractual dispute resulted in Britain receiving just three Lightnings. The remainder went to the USAAC as P-322s.

The first YP-38 made its maiden flight on 17 September 1940. Three days later a contract for sixty-six P-38 models was received, and on 30 August 1940 another contract for 410 Lightnings was issued. Deliveries of thirty-six P-38Ds to the Army Air Corps began in August 1941 and were followed by 210 P-38Es, 527 'F's, and 1082 P-28Gs. (P-38G-10-LO with two 165-US gallon drop tanks and four triple-cluster 4.5-inch rocket launchers, pictured).

XP-49 (Model 522, 40-762) stratospheric research aircraft which regularly flew above 40,000ft. This P-38 was modified to carry special supercharged Continental engines and was equipped with a pressurized cabin.

Heavy losses in the bomber groups in Europe made it obvious that long-range escort fighters would after all be required, and from mid-1942 the P-38F began to be deployed in large numbers. Pictured are P-38J-10-LO Lightnings of the 383rd FS, 364th FG, 8th AF (the nearest aircraft is 42-67978 *Betty III*), which flew their first fighter mission on 3 March 1944 from Honington, Suffolk.

P-38J-5-LO 42-67183, of which 375 were built, and F-5B-1-LO 42-67332 photographic version, in flight.

P-38L-5-LO 44-25419. The L was the final production version of the Lightning and 2,520 were built.

P-38L-5-LO fitted with underwing zero-length launchers for fourteen 5-inch HVAR. These proved unsatisfactory and were replaced with rocket 'trees' for ten 5-inch projectiles.

P-38M-5-LO 44-27234 two-seat Night Lightning was modified from P-38L-5-LO and included a SCR540 nose radome and launching racks for HVAR rockets beneath the wing. The type was successful and seventy-five P-38Ls were modified to P-38M standard.

F-5G-6-LO, the last photographic-reconnaissance version of the Lightning.

P-38 Photo-reconnaissance Lightning of the Italian Co-Belligerent Air Force, 1944.

XP-58 Chain Lightning (41-2670), an experimental escort fighter and anti-ship destroyer, one third larger than the P-38 and equipped with twin tail turrets and four 37mm high velocity cannon in the nose. Lack of suitable power plants resulted in the XP-58 not being flown until 6 June 1944, more than four years after design had begun.

Lockheed-Vega was one of three companies in the Boeing-Vega-Douglas (BVD) pool and turned out 2,750 Fortresses, 500 of them B-17Fs. Women workers played an invaluable role in building the aircraft and in this photo, a Rosie's Riveter adds the finishing touch to B-17F-15-VE 42-5764.

B-17E 41-2401 was modified by Vega with four 1,425hp Allison V-171089 liquid-cooled V-12 engines. Re-designated XB-38, it flew on 19 May 1943 and was faster than Wright-engined B-17s, but development was cut short when it crashed on 16 June after an engine caught fire.

B-17F-25-VE 42-5841 *Est Nulla Via In Via Virtutis*, flown by Lt Martin Andrews in the 423rd BS, 306th BG, which force-landed in Switzerland on 6 September 1943, was later test flown at the Emmen experimental centre, and at the end of the war was returned to the USAAF.

Vega built thirteen B-17Fs, FA701/713, for the RAF (FA711, pictured).

B-17F-1-BO (41-24341) was modified as an escort aircraft by Vega and became known as the XB-40 (pictured at Burbank on 10 November 1942 on the occasion of its first flight). The twenty Vega-built B-17Fs were modified by Douglas as YB-40 service-test models.

B-17G-5-VE 42-39871, is hoisted above other B-17s at Burbank. Of the 8,680 G models built by the BVD Pool factories, some 4,750, or more than one third of the total Fortress production, were lost on combat operations.

B-17G-5-VE 42-39843 joined the 364th BS, 305th BG, 8th AF, on 16 October 1943 and was named *Dailey's Mail*.

B-17G-15-VE 42-97525 *Invictus* in the 730th BS, 452nd BG, 8th AF, flying through flak. *Invictus* was lost on 8 March 1944 with 2/Lt Frank S. Stephens and crew.

56

B-17-15-VE 42-97504 OR-P *Mary Lou* in the 323rd BS, 91st BG, which crash-landed at Bassingbourn on 14 October 1944 following battle damage on the mission to Freiburg.

B-17-35-VE 42-5951, pictured during construction at the Vega plant early in 1943, reached the 353rd BS, 301st BG at Oudna, North Africa, in August 1943 and transferred to the 341st BS, 97th BG in December. On 23 June 1944 this B-17, named *Opissonya*, was shot down on the bomb run at Ploesti but the bombardier, 2/Lt David R. Kingsley, was still able to drop his bombs successfully. Kingsley was posthumously awarded the Medal of Honor.

B-17G-40-VE 42-97991 joined the 366th BS, 305th BG, 8th AF and was lost on 24 August 1944 on the mission to Merseburg.

B-17F-45-VE 42-6099 *Winnie C* of the 339th BS, 96th BG, 8th AF releases bombs on the Focke Wulf factory at Bremen on 26 November 1943. This Fortress failed to return with 2/Lt Nathan L. Young and crew on 22 March 1944.

B-17G-50-VE 44-8158 *Bobby Sox*, which served in the 490th and 94th Bomb Groups in England and the 15th AF in Italy.

B-17G-45-VE 44-8081 in the 731st BS, 452nd BG, 8th AF survived the war and was scrapped at Kingman, Arizona, in November 1945.

In 1946 two B-17G-VEs were used as test beds for new Wright and Pratt & Whitney propeller-turbine engines. The first (44-85813/BA-813) was acquired by the Wright Aeronautical Co. on a bailment contract as EB-17G (JB-17G in October 1956) to test the Typhoon propeller-turbine (pictured). The second (44-85734) was used at Hartford, Connecticut, to test the Pratt & Whitney XT-34.

After the war, Lockheed were called upon to produce another Boeing bomber design. The outbreak of the Korean War in 1950 resulted in a pressing need for more B-47 Stratojets and production was sub-contracted to both Douglas and Lockheed-Georgia. Eight B-47Bs were assembled from components built by Boeing-Wichita, and were followed by 386 B-47Es (B-47E-50-LM 52-3363, pictured) which were turned out at Marietta. In the late 1950s Lockheed Georgia converted fourteen RB-47Es to pilotless drones for use by the 3205th Drone Group at Eglin AFB.

Two
Transports, Trials and Tribulations

Model 1049H Super Constellation N1049H, operated by Dollar Airlines.

Lockheed were successful with their four-engined Model 49 airliner, for which the company had begun design studies in 1938. Pan American and TWA had shown initial interest and the Model 44 Excalibur, with accommodation for twenty-one passengers and a top speed of 241mph, evolved. This led in 1939 to a bigger and faster design, the Model 49 Constellation. TWA and Pan American each ordered forty Double Cyclone-powered Constellations but with the outbreak of war production switched instead to 180 C-69 long-range transports for the USAAF. The first aircraft, NX25600 (43-10309, pictured), was completed in December 1942 and first flew on 9 January 1943. Only fifteen C-69s were delivered, but these were followed by 233 civil airliner versions.

Model 049 N88861 of Pan American World Airlines, one of twenty-six Constellations purchased by Pan Am.

Model 049 PH-TET *Tilburg* of KLM, one of twenty-six Constellations obtained by the Dutch national airline.

Model 649 N101A of Eastern Airlines, which received fourteen Constellations from May 1947. It is fitted with a ventral pannier ('Speedpak') to carry up to 8,200lb of freight.

Constellation G-AMUP *Boston* of BOAC. The British airline bought just four Constellations (G-AHEK/AHEM & AHEN) direct from Lockheed.

With one eye on the post-war market, Lockheed brought out the Model 33 'Little Dipper' in 1944. Aimed at the fly-for-fun market, the Dipper was a one-place, low-wing monoplane with fixed tricycle landing gear. It was powered by a 50hp two-cylinder Air Cooled Motors engine and featured a bubble canopy and landing flaps. Although the war produced thousands of qualified pilots, when the war ended it also provided an excess of relatively inexpensive surplus aircraft and Lockheed turned its production efforts to other fields.

Lockheed also designed the Model 34 'Big Dipper' in anticipation of a boom in flying at the end of the war but this pusher-type, four-place aircraft never entered large scale production. It flew for the first time on 10 December 1945 but was lost in a landing accident on 6 February 1946. The engine was located in the fuselage aft of the passenger compartment and turned the propeller at the end of a shaft extending through the vertical stabilizer.

In 1946 Lockheed built two Model 75 Saturn aircraft to evaluate the possible demand for high-speed feeder airline or executive aircraft and the type first flew on 17 June 1946. The Saturn was found to be over-priced for the post-war commercial market which was flooded with far cheaper alternatives and the two prototypes were scrapped in early 1948.

Two huge 92-ton, double-decker XR60-1 (XR6V-1) Constitutions, each capable of carrying 180 persons, were constructed as Navy transports in 1946. The first of two XR60-1s (BuNo 85163) flew on 9 November 1946. Both aircraft were delivered to the Navy in 1949 but were found to be under-powered and to have insufficient range and the type never entered production.

Design work on the P2V (P-2) Neptune was begun in September 1941 but war intervened and the first XP2V-1 (26-1001) was not completed until the spring of 1945. It flew for the first time on 17 May that year but the end of the war saw orders for 100 cancelled. On 13 September 1946, however, Lockheed received an order for thirty P2V-2s and the onset of the Cold War and the Korean War saw an upsurge in orders that kept the aircraft in production until spring 1962. BuNo 89082 *The Turtle* (pictured), the first P2V-1, was modified during construction to attempt to set a new world distance record, which it did between 26 September and 1 October 1946.

Beginning in January 1952, Great Britain received fifty-two P2V-5s (designated Neptune MR.1s and serial numbered WX542/556) built with MDAP (Mutual Defense Assistance Program) funds and ordered under US Navy contracts. Neptunes entered service with No. 217 Squadron and also equipped Nos. 36, 203, and 210 Squadrons at Topcliffe (WX516 of No. 210 Squadron with characteristic remote-controlled search light is pictured).

The YP2V-7 prototype flew on 26 April 1954. P2V-7 BuNo 140964 (pictured) has the MAD (Magnetic Anomaly Detector) 'stinger' tail, twin .50 calibre guns in a dorsal turret, smaller ventral radome, and tip tanks. The P2V-7/P-2H was the final production version of the Neptune. Some P2V-7/P-2H Neptunes were later converted to P2V-7S/SP-2H and other variants.

A total of 1,051 Neptunes were built by Lockheed, including forty-eight assembled by Kawasaki, and eighty-two P-2Js also by Kawasaki (4,767 of the Japanese Self Defence Force, pictured).

C-69 (049-1961, NX25600) was converted to the Super Constellation prototype (1049-1961S, NX67900) by splicing new fuselage sections, fore and aft of the wing to increase its tourist-class seating by a third. It flew for the first time on 13 October 1950 and 579 Super Constellations followed off the production lines.

On 14 July 1950, the US Navy became the first military customer for the Super Connie when it placed an order for six PO-2W airborne-early warning aircraft, to be followed by orders for 202 more versions. Super Connies were operated by the US Navy (and USAF) for twenty-six years, from November 1952 to October 1978.

The US Navy obtained 142 WV-2 airborne early-warning aircraft, which in September 1962 were re-designated EC-121K under a new Tri-Service designation system.

Four R7V-2 (Model 1249A-95-75) transport versions of the Super Constellation were obtained by the US Navy. The first aircraft flew on 1 September 1954.

The RC-121D-LO (Model 1049A-55-86) was the main AEW version for the USAF, which obtained seventy-two Super Constellations for this role. In 1962 they were re-designated EC-121Ds.

Two YC-121F-LO (Model 1249A-94-75) transports (BuNos 131660, pictured, and 131661) were ordered as R7V-1 but were modified during construction as propeller-turbine-powered R7V-2s and delivered to the USAF as 53-8157 and 53-8158 respectively. They were operated by the Service Test Squadron (Turboprop) of MATS at Kelly AFB, Texas.

C-121C-LO (Model 1049F-55-96) USAF Transport version of the Super Constellation. Thirty-three (including 54-151, the first aircraft, pictured) were delivered to MATS in 1955 but ten were later modified to VC-121, JC-121 and EC-121 variants.

The WV-2E airborne electronic test bed (BuNo 126512) the first AEW aircraft to be fitted with a rotodome (containing antenna for the APS-82 radar), which first flew on 8 August 1956. In 1962 the WV-2E was re-designated EC-121L-LO.

Qantas introduced the Super Constellation into service in 1954. Model 1049E VH-EAD (pictured in January 1959) was one of sixteen Super Constellations operated by the Australian airline on their world routes.

Model 1049C VT-DGM of Air India, one of the first two Super Constellations bought by the airline. Eight more were purchased by the airline from Lockheed.

Model 1049G VT-DIL of Air India.

N1649, the prototype Model 1649 Starliner, which flew on 10 October 1956. The type could fly non-stop from New York to any European capital and went into service with TWA on the New York to Paris route on 1 June 1957. Some forty-three production models were built, twenty-nine being ordered by TWA, ten by Air France, and four by Lufthansa between 1957 and 1966.

The first prototype Jetstar (N329J) flew on 4 September 1957, just 241 days after design work had commenced. The C-140B-LM utility transport was the first military version to enter service with the USAF, in April 1961 (five were ordered), and these were soon followed by five C-140A-LM navaid-calibration aircraft. Four VC-140B-LO VIP transport versions (including 61-2489, pictured), based on the Jetstar 6, were also ordered.

The Jetstar 6 was designed with the corporate sector, non-military US Government agencies and foreign buyers in mind. The first production aircraft (N9201R) flew in the summer of 1966.

JetStar 6 CA103, one of three purchased for the Luftwaffe. Altogether a total of 204 two- and four-engined Jetstars, Nos 6 to 8 and 11, were built at Marietta.

Designed for short and medium routes, 170 Electra 188 prop-jet aircraft were built. N1881 was the first, flying on 6 December 1957. The Electra was quickly overtaken by the jet airliner revolution but in their short heyday they served fourteen major airlines on four continents.

Electra 188A N5502 of Eastern Airlines, the second of thirty-five Electras ordered by the airline. Eastern used its Electra fleet as back-up for Douglas DC-9s on the Boston-New York-Washington shuttle until 1977.

Model 188C VH-ECB of Qantas, in flight. The Australian airline purchased four of the Electras from Lockheed.

Electra N429NA of NASA pictured at Goose Bay.

The P-3 (P3V) Orion resulted from a Lockheed proposal in 1957 for maritime patrol development of the Electra airliner in response to a Navy requirement. The Lockheed proposal easily won the Navy competition and the YP3V-1 (modified third Electra) flew on 19 August 1958. An initial contract for seven P3V-1s in 1960 was followed by a production run of 150 P-3As (pictured).

P-3B KK-M, one of five Orions (c/n 185C-5301/5305) for Kongelige Norske Luftforsvaret (Royal Norwegian Air Force), in the markings of No. 333 Squadron.

P-3A 221-20 of the Ejército del Aire Español (Spanish Air Force), one of six ex-US Navy P-3As, serving with Escuadrón 221 at La Parra.

CP-140 (P-3C) 140110, one of 18 Auroras built for the Canadian Forces. A total of 611 Orions have been built, including four assembled in Japan and thirty-eight P-3Cs licence-built in Japan for the JMSDF.

The first YC-130-LO prototype (53-3396), which was to become famous as the Hercules, flew on 23 August 1954. The type was to become hugely successful, and is still in production. Some 204 C-130A-LM production versions followed (C-130A-LM 54-1625 with the original nose shape, pictured).

C-130A-LM 55-023 *City of Ardmore*, was the first of three in the first delivery to a Tactical Airlift Command operational squadron (463rd TAW), at Ardmore AFB, Oklahoma on 9 December 1956. The crew, from left to right: Joe Garrett, Captains Gene Chaney, Richard Coleman and T/Sgt Al Marchman, flight engineer.

Eighteen C-130A/JC-130As were modified as AC-130A gun-ships. The first of these, 53-3129, *The First Lady*, from the 919th SOG, 711th SOS based at Eglin AFB, Florida, first flew on 7 April 1955, and has had a remarkable career. It saw service in Vietnam, and was the oldest aircraft used in the Gulf War.

The C-130B-LM (Model 282) was the second production series of which 123 were built for the USAF, beginning in December 1958 (C-130B-LM 58-719 of Tactical Airlift Command, pictured). Thirty-three were delivered to Canada, Indonesia, Iran, Jordan, Pakistan and South Africa.

Twelve C-130D-LMs were ski-equipped versions for service in Alaska and Greenland (C-130D-LM 57-485 of Troop Carrier Command at the South Pole, pictured).

C-130B-LM 403, one of twelve Hercules acquired for the Royal South African Air Force, was delivered to No. 28 Squadron RAAF in November 1962.

The C-130E-LM (Model 382) was the third major production version, designed for longer-range logistic missions. The first C-130E flew on 15 August 1961 and 377 were delivered to the USAF while 109 went to nine overseas air forces (C-130E-LM 10305 of the RCAF, pictured).

The C-130H-LM version, which equips USAF, AFRES and ANG units, was first delivered to the Royal New Zealand Air Force in March 1965, and a further forty-one foreign military customers followed (C-130H-LM of Kongelige Norske Luftforsvaret (Royal Norwegian Air Force), pictured).

C-130H 74-2061 of the 435th Tactical Airlift Wing, Military Airlift Command, at Rhein-Main AFB, Frankfurt, Germany.

C-130H-LM of the Aeronautica Militare Italiana (Italian Air Force).

Forty-three HC-130H-LM (65-964 and 65-970 of Military Airlift Command, pictured) rescue and recovery aircraft were built for the USAF.

Another twenty-nine HC-130H-LM aircraft were delivered to the US Coastguard.

C-130H-LM of the USAF. In 1980 three USAF C-130Hs were fitted with an in-flight refuelling receptacle and downward-pointing braking rockets for possible use in the attempted rescue of hostages in Iran.

Fifteen HC-130N-LM search-and-rescue aircraft (69-5827 of Military Airlift Command, pictured), were built for recovery of aircrew and retrieval of space capsules.

GV-1 (KC-130F) 3022 of the US Marine Corps.

USMC C-130 (GV-1) 9816 refuelling two F-4 Phantoms of VMFA-232.

Sixty-six V-130K-LM models were purchased by Great Britain for the RAF (two C-130Ks, pictured, the nearest being XV191). The first flew on 19 October 1966 and, as the Hercules C. Mk 1, entered service with No. 242 OCU at Thorney Island in April 1967.

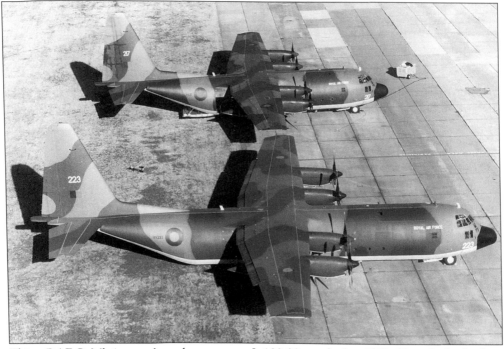

Thirty RAF C. Mk 1s were brought up to near L-100-30 standard in 1979-85, with the fuselage 'stretched' by 15ft, to give a near forty per cent increase in freight volume over the standard C-130. These were re-designated C. Mk 3s.

RAF Hercules W. Mk 2 *Snoopy* (XV208) was a modification by Marshall of Cambridge (Engineering) Ltd in 1967 for service with the Meteorological Research Flight at RAF Farnborough.

Nepalese children at Surkhet sift grain just brought to them by Hercules C-1 XV200 of No. 46 Group (RAF) Transport Command during the March 1973 Operation Khana Crusade in Nepal.

USAF C-130Hs of the 46th TAW, and two Hercules, XV293 and XV185, of 38 Group RAF, on the ramp at Moi International Airport, Mombasa, Kenya, late February 1993, during the humanitarian aid operation (Provide Relief/Restore Hope (US), Vigour (UK)) to Somalia. The RAF Hercules left for the UK on 1 March 1993.

L-100-30 of Southern Air Transport landing at Moi International Airport, Mombasa, February 1993, during the international relief effort 1992-93, to provide neighbouring Somalia with food, medicines and other essential supplies.

C-130E 62-1834, 435th Airlift Wing, piloted by 1/Lt Ross Becker (left) and 1/Lt Eric L. Meyers, *en route* from Rhein-Main, Frankfurt, Germany, to Sarajevo (UN Flight 17) on 23 March 1994 during Operation Provide Promise, the relief effort in Bosnia.

C-130H-LM 91-1231, the 2,000th Hercules built, at Split, Croatia, March 1994, being loaded with supplies for Bosnia, during Operation Provide Promise.

Safair L-100-30 ZS-JIZ during a test-drop of Snowdrop famine-relief sachets over the Piet Joubert Training Range, north of Pretoria, South Africa, 19 August 1993.

C-130 of the Blue Angels getting airborne with the assistance of JATO rockets.

RAF C-130K used to test the new Dowty R391 six-bladed propeller to be fitted to C-130J aircraft. The launch customer, the Ministry of Defence, placed an order for twenty-five C-130J-30 aircraft in late 1994; Italy has ordered eighteen, the RAAF twelve, and the USAF twenty-eight. By 1998 worldwide orders for standard and 'stretched' versions of the 'J' stood at eighty-three, with options for sixty-two more.

The Model 300 Starlifter jet transport was designed to replace the piston-engined and propeller-turbine-powered transports in the Military Air Transport Fleet and the first C-141A-1-LM (61-2775) flew on 17 December 1963.

C-141A-10-LM 63-8090 of the 1501st ATW, MATS, touching down.

Altogether, 285 C-141A Starlifters were built (C-141A-15-LM 64-622 pictured).

C-141-LM 65-247 at Butterworth, Malaya.

In one month during the Yom Kippur War in 1973, Starlifters flew 421 missions and delivered more than 10,000 tons of equipment and supplies to Israel. The operation highlighted an obvious need for increased airlift capability and an air refuelling facility, but budgetary restraints ruled out any new aircraft and so it was decided that the entire C-141 fleet would have to be 'stretched'. By inserting a 13ft 4in fuselage plug forward of the wing and a 10ft plug aft of the wing, usable volume was increased by almost seventy-five per cent, while a air refuelling boom receptacle was added atop the fuselage.

C-141A-LM 66-186, seen here demonstrating its air-to-air refuelling capability with a KC-135 tanker, was modified to become the YC-141B prototype and it first flew on 24 March 1977. All other existing C-141As were modified to C-141B configuration and the first production C-141B was accepted by MAC on 4 December 1979.

A wide-bodied transport with more than five times the capacity of the C-141A evolved because of the need to airlift the Army's M-60 tanks and CH-47 Chinook troop-carrying helicopters, which were too big for transporting in the C-141. In April 1965 USAF Systems Command considered five tenders for a CX-HLS (Cargo Experimental Heavy Logistics System) and opted for the Model 500 Galaxy. The first C-5A (66-8303) flew on 30 June 1968.

The first C-5A was followed by eighty-nine more Galaxies (68-222, pictured).

C-5A Galaxy 70-455 touching down.

The massive upward-lifting visor nose, which can be raised above the cockpit to enable the aircraft to taxi with the door open, and the loading ramp of the C-5A. The aft ramp is provided with clam-shell doors.

Four generations of Lockheed four-engined aircraft gathered at Harrisburg International Airport, home to the Pennsylvania Air Guard's 193rd Tactical Electronic Warfare Group's EC-121S-LO electronic reconnaissance/counter measures 'Super Connies' and C-130s. These two aircraft were joined by a C-141 and the C-5 Galaxy.

Lockheed's troubled L-1011 TriStar programme started promisingly in 1968 and the first aircraft flew on 15 September 1970. Some 250 TriStars were subsequently delivered, including G-BBAJ *Holyhead Bay* of British Air Tours (pictured at Faro, Portugal, in 1987).

TriStar of Millon Air (N851MA) lifting off from Marshalls Airport, Cambridge, after refurbishment.

TriStar *Stargazer* of CSC (N140SC) on finals at Cambridge.

Nine L-1011-500 airliners were acquired for conversion to RAF tankers for No. 216 Squadron. Six ex-British Airways TriStars were converted by Marshall Aerospace at Cambridge to K. Mk 1 tanker/passenger ZD950, ZD953, ZD951 and ZD949) and tanker/cargo (ZD948 and ZD952) transports, and three ex-Pan American TriStars became K. Mk 2 tanker/passenger aircraft (ZE704/706).

K. Mk 1 ZD951 with four Tornadoes, high over Alaska.

RAF TriStar ZD650 refuelling an RAF Hercules.

In the winter of 1966 the US Navy issued a requirement for a VSX (Experimental carrier-based ASW aircraft) and on 4 August 1969 the Lockheed YS-3A was declared the winner. The first of eight prototypes (BuNo157992) flew on 21 January 1972 and these were followed by 179 S-3A Viking production models (BuNo159410 of VS-22 with Texas Instruments AN/ASQ-81 magnetic anomaly detection (MAD) sensor in the extended retractable tailboom, pictured). The first S-3A Vikings joined VS-41 'Shamrocks' training squadron at NAS North Island, San Diego, California, in February 1974.

Three

Shooting for
the Stars

No fewer than 5,641 T-33As were built (T-33A-1-LO 51-4262, pictured) between 1948 and 1959.

XP-80-LO 44-85004 *Lulu Belle*, powered by a de Havilland Halford H.1B turbojet, flew for the first time on 8 January 1944, piloted by Milo Burcham. Six of the fourteen YP-80As were lost (Burcham was killed flying the third YP-80A on 20 October 1944), and by September 1946 some sixty-one aircraft had been involved in accidents. How ever, the P-80 Shooting Star went on to become undoubtedly the most successful of all the immediate post-war jet fighters to originate during the war, and the first to enter operational service. The last of 917 P-80As was delivered to the USAF in December 1946.

A total of 240 P-80Bs were delivered between March 1947 and March 1948, of which 117 were brought up to P-80C standard. The F-80B differed from the F-80A in having a thinner wing, an ejection seat, under-wing rocket launchers, new M-3 .50 calibre machine guns, and a 5,200lb thrust J33-A-21 engine with a water-alcohol injection system for bursts of emergency power. A total of 748 P-80C/F-80Cs were built and the last 561 aircraft (F-80C-10-LO 49-1820, pictured), were powered by a 5,400lb thrust J-33A-35 engine.

P-80C-5-LO 47-590 *Butch* pictured in Japan at the time of the Korean War. The F-80C was the last fighter version of the Shooting Star and could carry up to sixteen 5-inch rockets and either 'Misawa' wing tip tanks or 230-gallon Fletcher centreline tip tanks. Altogether, 1,732 Shooting Stars were built, including fifty TO-1s for the US Navy/USMC.

RF-80C 44-85260 *My Miss Carole B*, one of seventy F-80As modified to reconnaissance configuration, pictured in Japan at the time of the Korean War.

Lockheed added about 3ft to the fuselage of the F-80 to accommodate a second cockpit to produce the TF-80C and the world's first jet trainer. It flew for the first time on 22 March 1948 and on 5 May 1949 was renamed the T-33. The first production TF-80C was accepted by the USAF in August 1948. TF-80C-1-LO 49-987 is pictured in Japan at the time of the Korean War.

A decade after it was first introduced, ninety per cent of the free world's jet pilots were trained in the T-33. It equipped twenty-three friendly powers (about 1,058 aircraft), including several air forces in NATO. A total of eighty-five T-33As were modified to RT-33A configuration (RT-33A-1-LO 53-5587 of the Italian Air Force, pictured).

T-33A-1-LO (FT-05) of the 11ème Escadrille (11 Smaldeel), the Instrument Squadron of the Force Aérienne Belge.

T-33A-5-LO 58-575 of the USAF.

The US Navy received 699 TV-1/T2V-1 SeaStars, the first twenty-eight being designated TO-2s, carrier-based versions of the T-33B-LO.

The T2V1 (BuNo142261 pictured), had leading-edge slats fitted to the wing and a larger tail surface.

Between 1952 and 1959 Canadair built 656 CT-133AN Silver Stars (pictured), powered by a Rolls-Royce 5,100lb thrust Nene-10 turbo jet, and Kawasaki of Japan produced some 210 T-33As under licence. RT-33A reconnaissance versions and AT-33A light attack models were built before the Shooting Star finished its impressive career as QF-80 drones for missile targets, and DT-33A drone director aircraft.

Responding to an Air Force request for a two-man, all-weather fighter, Lockheed strengthened the T-33 fuselage and inserted an Allison J-33A turbojet with afterburner to create the YF-94. The first of two YF94 prototypes (48-356) flew on 1 July 1949 and production F-94As first entered service in June 1950. The 109 F-94As were followed by 355 F-94Bs (F-94B-1-LO 50-923 and 50-930, pictured).

F-94B-1-LO 50-882 in flight.

F-94B-5-LO 51-5355 pictured in Japan at the time of the Korean War.

110

F-94B-5-LO 51-5475. Some 279 F-94Cs followed, but a production order for 112 F-94Ds was cancelled after the YF-94 prototype was produced. All told, Lockheed built 854 Starfires, 1949-1854.

The experimental XF-90 (46-687), powered by two Westinghouse XJ34-WE-11 turbojets, was designed as a long-range penetration aircraft and first flew on 3 June 1949. The needle-nosed jet lost out to the McDonnell XF-88 in June 1950 and therefore did not enter production.

The US Navy XFV-1 was designed to rise vertically, level off for swift, horizontal flight, and land on its tail wheels by hanging suspended by contra-rotating propellers geared to a single, Allison XT-40-A (twin T38 turbine) engine. The XFV-1 first flew on 16 June 1954. The research programme was concluded in 1955 after providing much valuable data for military consideration on VTOL aircraft.

Military testing of the VZ-10 (XV-4) Hummingbird VTOL aircraft began on 28 May 1963 when the first of two prototypes (XV-4A 62-4503) made its maiden flight. In February 1964 this aircraft, and XV-4B 62-4504, were handed over to the US Army but 4503 was lost in an accident and the second aircraft was given to NASA for wind-tunnel testing before being placed in storage.

112

The XF-90, XFV-1 and XV-4 fighter concepts never entered production but the XF-104 programme more than compensated for them. The Starfighter saga began with two XF-104-LOs (Model 083-92-01) (53-7786/7787), which were followed by a batch of seventeen YF-104-LOs (Model 183-93-02, including 55-2969, pictured), built for service trials with the General Electric J79-GE-3 engine. Mach 2 was achieved in a YF-104 on 27 April 1955.

F-104A-5-LO (Model 183-93-02) 56-737 of Air Defense Command in flight. Deliveries of the F-104A to the 83rd Fighter-Interceptor Squadron at Hamilton AFB, California, began on 26 January 1958.

F-104A-5-LO, 10-LO, and 15-LO (Model 183-93-02) Starfighters in formation. From top down: 56-748, 56-737, 56-766, and 56-772.

F-104A-15-LO 56-777 and three F104A-20-LO Starfighters, 56-805, 808, and 810, in formation near the Bay bridge, San Francisco.

F-104C-5-LO 56-883 in flight high above the Mojave Desert, California. The single seat 'C' tactical strike version and two-seat 'D', were developed for use by Tactical Air Command and deliveries of seventy-seven F-104Cs were made between 16 October 1958 (to the 831st Air Division at George AFB, California) and June 1959. On 14 December 1959 an F-104C took the world altitude record to 103,389ft.

Four F-104C-5-LOs of the 479th TFW in flight. 56-908 is fitted with a removable in-flight refuelling probe. For nuclear strikes an MK-28 special store could be carried beneath the fuselage.

F-104C-5-LO Starfighter 56-904 of the 479th Tactical Fighter Wing at George AFB, California. During the Cuban Missile Crisis the 479th TFW were stationed at Key West, Florida.

Line-up of Canadian CF-104, USAF F-104A-20-LO, and Fiat-built Luftwaffe F-104G (KC-101/104) Starfighters. Canadair built 200 CF-104s (CL-90) and 140 F-104Gs as part of the Mutual Assistance Program. Fiat built 444 F-104G and S Starfighters.

CF-104 60770 in flight. The first Canadair CF-104 was airlifted to Palmdale, California, where it was first flight-tested by Lockheed on 26 May 1961.

The F-104G-LO (Model 683-10-19) was by far the most important Starfighter version and resulted from a competition, won by Lockheed in October 1958 against eight other aircraft types, to supply the Luftwaffe with a multi-role, all-weather aircraft. West Germany received 915 Starfighters made up of 262 from Lockheed, and 653 from the North, South, West and Italian Groups, and MBB.

Luftwaffe F-104Gs in formation with Harriers of RAF Germany. Over thirty-five per cent of all Starfighters built served the West German Air Force. Altogether, 1,127 Gs were built, or forty-four per cent of Starfighter production.

TF-104G N104L (Model 583D) was initially retained by Lockheed as a company demonstrator. It was used by Jacqueline Cochran to set world records and in May 1965 was delivered to the Koninklijke Luchtmacht (KLu or Royal Dutch Air Force) with the Dutch serial, D-5702.

TF-104G-LO two-seat trainer of the Kongelige Norske Luftforsvaret (Royal Norwegian Air Force).

The Aeronautica Militare Italiana (AMI) received 125 Fiat-built F/RF-104Gs and 24 Lockheed-built TF-104Gs and in 1986 was the largest user of Starfighters with eleven squadrons of F-104s. The first Lockheed-modified F-104S advanced all-purpose Starfighter was flown in December 1966 and Fiat built 246 F-104Ss for the AMI (pictured) and Turkish Air Force.

Fiat-built F-104G KC104 of the Luftwaffe and RCAF, and 16-8501, one of three F-104Js built by Lockheed for the Koku Jieitai (Japanese Self Defence Force). The three Js were followed by twenty-nine assembled by Mitsubishi from Lockheed components, and 178 were built by Mitsubishi.

The Greek Elliniki Vassiliki Aeroporia (Royal Hellenic Air Force) received thirty-five F-104Gs and four TF-104Gs; nineteen and six more respectively were transferred from other countries to make up attritional losses.

TF-104G-LO D-5812, one of thirteen built by Lockheed for the Koninklijke Luchtmacht. Four more were co-produced by Lockheed and Fokker.

Fokker-built RF-104G D-8145 of the Koninklijke Luchtmacht (KLu or Royal Dutch Air Force). The North Group (its leader, Fokker) built 119 of these tactical reconnaissance versions of the Starfighter.

Fokker-built F-104G D-8341 of the Koninklijke Luchtmacht. Altogether, 350 Starfighters were built by the North Group for the KLu and Luftwaffe, 231 of these being F-104Gs.

SABCA-built F-104Gs of the Force Aérienne Belge (FAeB, or Belgian Air Force). The West Group, with SABCA as leader, and Avions Fairey, flew its first F-104G on 3 August 1961, and built a total of 188 Starfighters for the FAeB and the Luftwaffe.

Eighteen C.8 and three CE.8 Starfighters (Canadair-built F-104Gs and Lockheed TF-104Gs respectively) served with the Ejército del Aire (Spanish Air Force) from March 1965 to May 1972. These Starfighters are from Escuadrón 161 at Torrejón. In 1972 all Spanish Starfighters were returned to the USAF for transfer to Greece and Turkey.

CF-104 (12706), one of 200 Starfighters produced by Canadair for the RCAF/Canadian Armed Forces. Starfighters equipped eight Canadian squadrons in Europe from 1962, and the last aircraft were phased out in 1986 when 441 Squadron replaced its CF-104s with CF-18 Hornets.

The U-2 high-altitude strategic and weather reconnaissance aircraft was designed amid great secrecy by Kelly Johnson and his team to meet a requirement from the Department of Defense for a USAF reconnaissance aircraft capable of operating over the Soviet Union at sub-sonic speeds at altitudes above 70,000ft. The first U-2 flew on 4 August 1955 at the secret base at Groom Lake in the Nevada desert. Altogether, forty-eight U-2As (55-6675/6722) were built (55-6703, pictured). The twenty-five U-2Rs that were built were deliberately much bigger and far heavier than the earlier U-2C, which, because of its low wing loading, had been prone to over-speed problems.

A U-2B flown by Lt Francis Gary Powers, one of several 'sheep-dipped' pilots (ex-military pilots 'recruited' by the CIA) was shot down near Sverdlovsk by a SA-2 SAM on a CIA-sponsored 'Operation Overflight' from Peshwar to Bodo, Norway, on May Day 1960. For almost four years, starting in July 1956, twenty-nine previous secret missions had gone unchallenged by the Soviet Union. Powers survived and was tried. In February 1962 he was exchanged for the US-based Soviet spy, Colonel Abel. Powers' U-2 is now on display in Moscow (pictured).

Full design go-ahead for a batch of twelve single-seat A-12 Mach 3-plus reconnaissance aircraft was given to Lockheed on 30 January 1960. This was later increased to fifteen plus nine two-seat drone carriers. The first A-12 (60-6924) flew on 26 April 1962. YF-12A-00-LO (60-6934), the first of three interceptor versions, flew on 7 August 1963. 60-6936, pictured, was the third YF-12A, which flew on 13 March 1964. The YF-12As initially were assigned to the 4786th Test Squadron at Edwards AFB.

Col. Robert L. 'Fox' Stephens and Lt Col. Daniel Andre who on 1 May 1965 in 60-6936 set three world records, including a world speed record of 2,070.12 mph. 60-6936 crashed on 24 June 1971 at Edwards AFB.

The SR-71A version of the A-12 first flew on 22 December 1964. (Note the extended fuselage chines, which contribute lift and control as well as providing space for some of the fuel and equipment). Thirty-one SR-71As (64-17950/80) plus one SR-71A(C) hybrid, built from salvaged parts, were built (64-17961, the twelfth SR-71A, pictured) before production ceased in 1968. The Blackbird is the world's most advanced strategic reconnaissance aircraft, powered by two J58 turbojets and capable of more than three times the speed of sound. It can survey over 100,000 square miles in one hour from an altitude of 80,000ft.

A SR-71A dramatically ignites fuel during a fly-by at the Mildenhall Air Fête. Built almost entirely of titanium to withstand external skin temperatures of between 450°F and 1,100°F, the Blackbird is also coated with high-emission black paint to radiate away stored heat.

In 1994 work began on the U-2 fleet of thirty-five single seat and two two-seat trainers, to retro-fit them with a derivative of the engine used in the Northrop B-2A *Spirit*. This has resulted in a 1,200lb weight reduction and a fuel saving of more than fifteen per cent. The first three U-2S versions were delivered to the USAF on 28 October 1994.

A 20ft titanium tailpipe for a U-2S being attached to a FE-118-GE-101 engine at Palmdale in October 1994. The USAF received funds from NASA to incorporate two NASA-owned ER-2 aircraft into the Air Force re-engining programme and conversion began late in 1996. The engine and other upgrades, such as a new emergency start system and electrical generator systems, are expected to extend the service life of the U-2 to the year 2020.

Not until the 1990s did Lockheed return to fighter designs. The F-117A was the first production combat type designed to exploit low-observable (LO) technology. Development and manufacture (starting with five full-scale development F-117As) began simultaneously in November 1978 within a highly classified environment. The fifty-ninth and final production aircraft was delivered on 12 July 1990 (F-117A-18 82-01802, pictured; sixty were built, but the first crashed before USAF acceptance and is not counted).

The existence of the F-117A was not revealed officially until November 1988, and its first operational deployment was to Panama just after midnight on 20 December 1989 when six F-117As supported Operation 'Just Cause'. During the Gulf War, starting on 17 January 1991, more than forty F-117A Nighthawks undertook 1,270 missions, attacking top-priority targets.